Get What YOU Want from Your Man

A Guide to Creating the Relationship You DESERVE

Shirley Baldwin

NEW YORK

LONDON • NASHVILLE • MELBOURNE • VANCOUVER

Get What You Want From Your Man

© 2019 Shirley Baldwin

Published in New York, New York, by Morgan James Publishing in partnership with Difference Press.
www.MorganJamesPublishing.com

The Morgan James Speakers Group can bring authors to your live event. For more information or to book an event visit The Morgan James Speakers Group at www.TheMorganJamesSpeakersGroup.com.

ISBN 978-1-68350-983-7 paperback
ISBN 978-1-68350-984-4 eBook
Library of Congress Control Number: 2018934574

Cover Design by:
Rachel Lopez
r2c design
r2cdesigns.com

Interior Design by:
Megan Whitney Dillon
Creative Ninja Designs
megan@creativeninjadesigns.com

In an effort to support local communities, raise awareness and funds, Morgan James Publishing donates a percentage of all book sales for the life of each book to Habitat for Humanity Peninsula and Greater Williamsburg.

Get involved today! Visit
www.MorganJamesBuilds.com

For Jeff

Without you, none of this would have been possible. Thank you for allowing me to be me and loving me anyway. For believing in me when I didn't believe in myself, continuously pushing me to be better, letting me feel what real love feels like, and showing me that all of this is possible. Together we are limitless. You're my best friend, partner, lover, monster, and constant support. You are my peace and my bliss. I love you.

Content

Foreword

Every once in a while, a book comes along that just hits you square in the belly, a book that is strong and impactful and in which every word seems to jump off the page. Shirley Baldwin's *Get What You Want from Your Man* is one of those books. The distance between the genders and how to bridge it isn't an easy conversation, but Shirley skillfully guides you through the steps necessary to unlock your hidden potential and create lasting happiness between you and your mate. This reflective how-to book is personal, straightforward, and reveals simple strategies for understanding fundamental communication problems common to most relationships.

Whether your issues are emotional disconnect or bottling up your feelings, the steps herein will bring peace and balance to what may seem like hopeless dysfunction. Shirley shows many simple strategies for improving many of the unresolved feelings most of us have experienced. No matter how much time passes, no couple wants to drift to the point that they seem like complete strangers to each other, to let a bond once forged in love and passion slowly slip and diminish away.

We are, most of us, subject to a multitude of ideologies, social influences, and many other external factors that negatively affect our ability to effectively communicate – and yet that ability to communicate how we think and feel is fundamental to having more open, honest, and meaningful relationships. The ways in which we communicate as men and women are of course different, depending on the programming we receive as children and in our learning experiences. But, as Shirley explains, we are all fundamentally searching for the same things, and can effectively shift our reality with just a shift in perception in order to bring it into alignment with what we desire.

When I first met Shirley, I could tell she had magic in her spirit. This book is a true, living testimony of overcoming personal struggles and changing focus, all the while creating healthy change and good communication skills. Shirley uses a variety of examples from her personal past as well as her work to hold out hope. Even when all seems lost and our relationships feel broken, there is always a way to repair the connection. And, of course, Shirley exemplifies what I and men who pay attention have always known: it is you, you women, who hold the power.

That said, it takes two to tango, and Shirley shows us all of us, men and women, how to better facilitate and serve each other as partners, lovers, and friends. Simple ways of finding solutions and reconciliation through vulnerability (and in trust), so that we can all learn to be better communicators. A personal motto of mine is, "Create comfort in your own discomfort." It's all in the brain, the mindset, in how we choose to not only see the world spin, but also our partnership with the people in it. We all experience struggles in learning how to better communicate in our own personal relationships. As Shirley explains, it's not always pleasant, comfortable, or easy to step into our power, but doing so impacts how we show up, and how we handle adversity and conflict. The more honest and heartfelt we are, the more we achieve clarity and understanding of where our partners are coming from.

Continue to push, adapt, acknowledge your perspective, and always come from a place of love. Let your love burn bright, and share it with others. I know this book will go on to help many others, as it has me.

Joe Anglim
Los Angeles, California
October, 2017

Introduction
On Wanting and Needing More from Your Husband

I was talking to my friend Jenny recently about marriage – and divorce. She said, "We were married 16 years and I really thought we had it made when we passed the seven-year mark. Guess I thought wrong."

Jenny is like a lot of women I know. She's probably like you. After close to a couple of decades of being married and raising kids, she'd moved past the taking-care-of-everyone-else stage. But when she woke up to wondering where her own dreams had gone, she realized she'd simply forgotten to fulfill them. She felt empty, incomplete, isolated–and she blamed her husband.

Maybe you are having these thoughts. Maybe you are blaming your husband, too. Who are you now, after all these years as a couple? Where did your dreams go? Who is that person you're married to, and what happened to the guy you met? He doesn't seem to come home much anymore. When he does, he seems unhappy about it. Doesn't help around the house much, doesn't appreciate all you do to keep the home running. Seems to only care about getting his own needs met. His friends and work take priority. You can't shake the resentment. Is this you?

Could be that the kids are older and leaving home, or conversely, maybe you still have young ones that take so much of your energy and headspace. He has no idea what you deal with on a daily basis. There doesn't seem to be much in common between you anymore. You want to talk to him about it, but based on your past attempts, you conclude he won't care, so you just continue to get by each day, honestly not knowing how much longer you can take it. You want more from him. More support, more investment, more care – more unconditional *love*.

I know this story. I've lived it. I've felt the pain and hopelessness. Although it's supposedly common, you feel completely alone while you're in it. The idea of taking back your life and relationship, and feeling happy and powerful again, sounds *so good*. Come with me on this journey. I've walked this path. I know the way out of the hopeless place and into the light and the joy that your married life can still be – if you choose to believe.

Chapter One
Everything I Learned About Men, the Long Way

I spent most of my life *hating* men. I felt they were selfish, disrespectful, and just plain out to get women. Confusingly, I also knew that it was a natural part of life to develop relationships with the opposite sex, and even to want those relationships to last. Lots of us carry contradictions.

I grew up like a gypsy, one of seven kids in a family with no money who was always on the move to find the next job. Making friends was difficult; sometimes we'd only live somewhere for a few months before moving again. I'm starting to lose count, but as of now, I believe I am living in my 55th house in my

46 years on this earth. I bonded as best I could to each new group of friends, each new set of neighbors and classmates and possibilities, trying to always smile and say "hi" to everyone. I knew we would be gone shortly, so it was inevitable that some of my relationships would be shallow and short-lived. Others, I grabbed onto with a kung-fu-like grip, trying to get close as fast as I could before I had to let them go.

I was a smart, observant child, and I took in everything around me. I had gifts that most people didn't have, but to me, the way I operated was the norm. I could read people from a very young age. I could tell if they were what I thought of as "good" or "bad," and then, as I grew, I learned that there were a lot more nuances than just those two broad categories. I ended up on my own at age 15 due to a difference in religious beliefs between my parents and me. That's when I went from being pretty well-protected – i.e. forbidden to step outside on my own – to living on the streets for a time. I was in survival mode for sure, but I got through the experience by imagining a fantasy life, one in which I felt safe, met my true love, and lived happily ever after. Like lots of American women raised on fairy tales, I needed a man to ride me off into the sunset on his white horse and take care of me.

Shortly after I moved out, I became involved with a man who was then my boss. He was 28, I was 15. Not appropriate, but

I didn't know better at the time. Even though I was an intelligent child, I couldn't see that the age difference alone wasn't a good recipe for a healthy relationship. I was still a child and I was essentially playing house, but it all felt grown up and safe for a bit. But there was no white horse, and no happily ever after, not even an alluring sunset. There was some abuse involved, and I was forced to grow up pretty quick. From that relationship, I developed issues with my looks, my weight, and my worth. This man would blame me for his actions, control the food I ate, and constantly correct my words, my thoughts, everything about me. He was super-critical of everything: my cooking, how I cleaned, how I did laundry. He would go on dates with other women during that time, and then come home to tell me about how they went. He was even dating a good friend of mine sometime during the process. It wasn't a secret, but all of us were unhealthy enough that we allowed it to happen anyway.

He had a six-year-old child that I was acting as part-time mom to. I still worked for him and essentially ran three of his businesses, although I was never paid any type of wage for the work I was doing. By the time I was 17, I had a ton of business knowledge, which I can't help but be grateful for today. I think back to that relationship and realize that what little foundation of self-confidence and self-respect I did have, after leaving my parents' home and our chaotic family life, was completely rocked and cracked – and it took me years after my escape from him to repair the damage.

Your story is probably – thankfully – not as dark as mine, but I wanted to share this part of my past so early in this narrative because it was a turning point for me – and one of the reasons I hated men. I projected, on all men, this one man's terrible behavior. Is there a certain situation in your background that created incredibly negative feelings towards men?

After that relationship, I dated around a little. It wasn't long before I met the first man that I would marry. He was 32 and by then I was 19. He was kind, and we were good friends. We were married for a dozen years, and from that marriage we had three kids – Kenzi, Carter, and Graycee. Life was pretty good, but we didn't have much passion or deep connection, nor did we have much in common besides our kids. I was young and lacked self-confidence, for one. I didn't know much about how to treat a man, since my mom had been pretty unhappy and harsh with my dad. My only significant relationship to that point had been one of exploitation, slavery, and service. So I just existed and tried to be the best person I could be, which was a good friend, a good mom, and a good housekeeper. My kids were my everything, and I loved being a mom. Not a day went by that I wasn't fulfilled and grateful. I put all of my being into mothering.

Do you feel like this in your relationship? Like the days just pass and they're ok, but nothing fabulous or extraordinary? Like you and your husband are just co-existing? On reflection, I am sure that had I known what I know today, my first marriage would have never ended. At the time, I just didn't know any better, about how to get the best from myself, or my marriage.

In my next relationship, I moved on to a completely opposite personality, thinking maybe that was the problem. I was practicing and teaching kung fu and this man was one of my instructors. This one was younger than I, by four years. Again, we didn't have a ton in common, but we did end up marrying and having a child, Saber, and I tried hard to make it all work. My second husband had addiction problems, lied often, and didn't seem to actually like me. I didn't feel safe with him, but I was really invested in making it work. Maybe a little too invested. We tried to merge our differences. I thought that if I just loved him enough, he would change. Spoiler alert, he didn't – I didn't yet realize that people do not change just because their partner really wants them to – so after six years, I was gone, without resolve or answers and carrying with me a little more animosity towards men. I look back now and realize that it wasn't all him. That I still had a lot to learn.

During the next year or so after we broke up, I stayed single. I was super happy, grew a lot as a person, had a good job, supported my kids, and continued to play Supermom. I was working alongside men every day, specifically in major league baseball, and I constantly pumped them for answers to my "guy questions," trying to figure what men were all about. I spent hours on end asking everything I could think of. Although I dated around a bit during this time, I felt that I didn't need a man, since I had all of these friends in my life. Moreover, I never wanted to experience the pain of another failed relationship. I told myself everything was all good.

Then a friend introduced me to the man who would become my next husband. She had told me that he was "a good one." He shared my religious values as well as marriage and life goals, really liked me, had custody of his two children, and was also willing to take on my four kids. He seemed like the perfect catch – or so I thought. From that period where I chose to stay single and work on me, I had developed a lot more confidence, was somewhat independent, and didn't feel like I *needed* a man. At the time, I figured I was in good shape to start a new relationship. I had also learned so much about giving to, and loving, a man – at least in my mind. I wasn't angry toward men. There was no way this one wouldn't work.

We were married within five months. *This was the one that was supposed to work*. I thought I had figured out how to be successful in a relationship. I gave everything of myself. Immediately after marriage, I started finding out things about him that, had I known going in, I wouldn't have accepted in the first place. My third husband had me believing if I just kept treating him like a king, we would be good. Old fears and feelings came back. All the work I had done on myself, my self-confidence, my clear head – the entire package started to unravel.

I was married to a man who was very controlling, yet passive-aggressive about it. He messed with my mind and had me feeling crazy most of the time. Except I was determined to not have another divorce. There was constant contention in our home, and he seemed to enjoy it. More time was spent disagreeing and trying to win than having peace or sharing experiences. So much time was wasted on that. I changed, and not for the better: in this relationship, I became super anxious, jealous, frequently ill, and not myself. I wanted to control how he treated me, how he behaved with other women, even how he saw things. I wanted to be his conscience, which is impossible of course. I wanted to "make" him love me the way I needed to be loved. This was super unhealthy, to believe we can change the way another thinks or behaves, just as it is to want any type of control over another person. It didn't work. My effort to change the way he treated me only created more problems between us. We were married for a total of eight years, and by the time it ended, I was exhausted, ill, had lost myself. It doesn't matter if you're in a relationship with someone who is toxic, like I was, or with someone who you may do well with, but for your own bad habits. Controlling another human, or feeling like you should be able to change one if you try hard enough, never turns out well.

This was not only the end of my third marriage, it was the end of me trying to pretend that I could control my husband – any husband. Over the next year, I researched and studied, and questioned how I came to think and behave the way I thought and behaved, and I finally got myself on track. I got clear that you can't change another person, but when you come from a place of love, a healthy foundation, and respect, you can *influence* that person to *want* to change. This was a difficult thing to learn for me – it took me many years and three marriages! But finally, I learned to release the blame and resentment I'd been feeling toward men in general, forgive and accept my own journey, and realize that I had a lot more control than I thought. That control is within me. I can only control *how I'm being* in the relationship, which includes what I am accepting and tolerating from someone else.

I really wanted my next relationship, if there was going to be one, to be different. I actually started dating Jeff shortly after my third divorce. We had been very close friends for quite a while, and found we were much alike in so many ways. We had both worked on ourselves sincerely over the preceding year and felt like we could take on anything together. Not saying that it has all been easy in our relationship, but when two people can speak the same language, understand one another's perspective, and use the proper tools for relating and communicating, they can get through the toughest of times. And we have, in a really beautiful way. Each trial and obstacle has brought learning, growth, and more understanding, and our love has grown stronger. I've watched this man shift in ways I never thought possible. I am going to show you over the next few chapters the practices that have had a tremendous effect on my ability to create what I want in my relationship.

Interestingly, when I started writing this book, Jeff said to me, "In a way I feel like you're writing your playbook on me, and it's a bit uncomfortable. In another way, I love it because I believe in it and it works. I'm fulfilled and happy and I want to do the same for you." (To see Jeff's perspective on why my relationship techniques work, read his letter to you at the end of this book.)

My journey hasn't been easy, nor did all of this understanding and awareness come quickly. By the time I went through the last divorce, I was 46 years old. I had been taken advantage of so many times and had made more mistakes of my own than I can count along the way. I've been to counseling, life coaching, zoning, retreats, muscle testing, chakra clearing, energy healing, and EFT. I've taken more behavioral sciences classes than I can count. Even got certified in a few of these modalities, for more understanding.

I've personally coached hundreds of individuals, including professional athletes and celebrities, worked alongside experts both in the coaching and psychological industries, listened to podcasts, explored blogs, and read a plethora of self-help books. I've held some clients' and friends' hands while they saved their marriages – and other clients' and friends' hands as they dissolved them. It wasn't until the end of my last marriage that I started to really put everything that I had learned together and made sense of it all for myself, at a high and repeatable level. I finally figured out how to *be* in a relationship that serves you, serves your man, and gives you space to create everything you've ever wanted.

You might be asking how I, a three-time divorcee, am in a position to give any kind of advice on relationships. The answer is this: *It's my calling.* I've been through it, and through more of it again. I have failed and walked through painful circumstances so that others may succeed. I have learned from the mistakes I made and the situations I was given to learn from. I know what works and what doesn't. In recent years, through my work as a coach, I've seen my program work again and again. This book will help you see the world through a man's eyes –*your* man's eyes. Everything will be amplified and rendered clearer, simpler, more attainable. If I can help one woman – maybe even you – embrace your womanhood, shift the heart of your man, and feel empowered to save your marriage, I will feel I've done my part. I believe this work is the most important work I can do on this planet and will affect generations to come.

But wait, you're saying. *There's nothing wrong with* me. He's *the one who needs to change!* And you're not wrong. Let's start off right where you are, right now, where I was not so very long ago. What the heck is *wrong* with him, anyway!? Read on and find out.

Chapter Two

What in the World Is Wrong with Him?

I f you are reading this book, you are probably at a point where something needs to happen. You have needs too, and they need to be met. In this lifetime. You feel like you're on a merry go round in a relationship stuck in dysfunction, and it isn't stopping anytime soon.

He can't seem to understand you, or discern what you want or need from him. Is it a bigger house, a new car, a diamond ring? Could it simply be more understanding, good conversation, quality time? What about safety, security, fidelity, the feeling of being the most important thing to him? How about help with the kids, help around the house, wanting to be romanced and made to feel beautiful? Do you want to be heard and appreciated? The list goes on and on. I've heard a lot of the same things from the women I work with – these are some very common gaps in our relationships and marriages.

Simply put, you want more from your man. Instead, he seems to be selfish and self-centered. Makes it all about him. Can't see beyond his need for sex, or maybe his ego needs regular attention, too. Loves being with his guy friends, at work, in the garage, or in front of the TV, more than being with you. Never seems to listen, doesn't care, likes to be critical, and doesn't appreciate you or all you do for him. Views you as his least priority. Wants you to change and be more accepting of him and his manly ways. Sound like your man? These are also some common complaints and frustrating behaviors I hear from the women I work with. What's wrong with all of these guys, anyway? Who raised these fools?

One of my first clients, Veronica, came to me distraught. Her marriage was on the rocks, and she didn't know what to do. She had heard about me from a friend, and she came in search of help with virtually no knowledge of who I was or how I worked, just pure desperation. I remember hearing her out on our first session and feeling like I already knew her. I had experienced what she was feeling. I knew how to help her, and I was so excited to be able to tell her that. She got to the end of her story, I gave her a tissue, and then I said, "I can help you." I watched her body visibly relax into the loveseat in my office, and I knew at that moment that she was all in, because, finally, there was some reason to have hope.

Veronica was a strong woman. She was raised by a single mom with her brother, at least since Veronica was five and her brother was three. Her mom worked two jobs and made sure that they had everything they needed. All by herself. As Veronica got older, she had to take up much of the slack while her mom was away at work. She was controlling and bossy toward her brother, because that's the only way he would listen to her. She stayed in the house with her mom until her brother left for college, when it felt like it was finally OK for her to move on with her life.

She soon met a boy named James and fell in love with him. They dated for a year and a half, and on the following Christmas Eve, he proposed to her. She was finally going to have the fairy tale life that she had always dreamed of! The perfect marriage, three or four kids, a family dog, and a house with a white picket fence around it. She wanted it all, her dreams were big.

Everything she had seen on TV, and all the things that her mom should have had and could never provide. She couldn't wait to start this new, wonderful life.

Eight years into it, Veronica was crying in my office, hopelessly frustrated and disillusioned – that happily ever after sure isn't what she thought it would be. Sure, she had the husband, the three kids, even had one extra dog. No picket fence – and no fairy tale, that's for sure.

She focused her irritation on her husband and her day-to-day, ho-hum life. It was quiet in the suburbs. Boring! She really wanted him to change. Why couldn't he just lift a finger once in a while? Why couldn't he take some initiative? Why wouldn't he take her on a romantic getaway? Or surprise her with that bracelet she has been wanting for so long? Why couldn't he just spend time with her and talk to her in the evenings? What was wrong with him? Her needs were important. Why couldn't he just see that he needed to do something about all of this?

What Veronica and I created over the next few months, in terms of a shift, was beautiful. I took her step-by-step through each session and covered several core relationship areas that in her and James' case were pretty lacking. I showed her a different way to see herself, and a different way to see her man. I taught her how to communicate with him, and how she could actualize more power and influence in her relationship. I taught her how he thinks, what his needs are, why he is behaving so differently than she does. She learned how to be a certain way in her relationship so that her man enjoyed being with her, and was willing and happy to give her all that she needed and wanted. She learned how to motivate and influence him, without ever saying a thing about it. *Pretty powerful.*

Since Veronica, I've had many more clients work with me to resolve similar issues in their marriages. Now, these women have husbands and significant others who happily give them what they want. They have relationships that work for them and everyone is fulfilled. These women have completely different views of their men than they did before. They have embraced the powerful woman inside of themselves, and use *her* to influence whatever they want to create in their relationships. I am seeing these couples thrive and grow closer together all the time. This was the result Veronica had, and the result you can have too.

What I taught Veronica and the others is exactly what I am going to teach you in this book. I will take you on a journey of discovery, understanding, and love. I can't wait to see how you emerge. At the end of the book, there are links and instructions to go to my website, so you can let me know how it turns out. I'd love to hear from you.

Chapter Three

It's a Matter of Perspective

*"When you change your perspective,
you change your reality."*

J ust as I recounted my frustrated female clients' usual laundry list of faults they find with their men, I have found that the men tend to hold common, stereotyped perspectives on women. They refer to women as high maintenance, moody, expensive, crazy, manipulative, controlling, and gold diggers. In fact, I just saw a live video this week where a woman wouldn't give the time of day to a man while he was dressed as a skinny hipster, driving an old Prius, but then he went and changed his clothes and drove up in a limo – and she was all over him. It's women like that who make the rest of us look bad. All of these are just perspectives that these individuals have gathered from their experiences, added their own opinions, and put a label on top.

Starting with some awareness and curiosity, with regards to your perspectives, will help you notice how they manifest in every area of your life. Most of the time we're not aware of what they are, and we allow our perspective to develop without individual ownership. Which means we experience situations that validate that perspective, which we may not even intend. We absorbed it from our upbringing, from the five people we associate most with, or some other influences without thinking. We all know how that works in other areas. For instance, if we focus on the negative, that's what we are going to see. If your intentional – or even wholly unconscious and unintentional – perspective is to see your man as selfish, then you will be able to find ample evidence of it several times a day. Anything he does for himself will seem selfish, even self-care or interruptions of his attention – such as going to the gym, or taking a moment to look at his phone – when you have part of your brain always tuned in to looking for the proof.

In contrast to that, if you intentionally seek the positive from your man, you will start to see more positive things about him. With that perspective, his decision to spend Saturday morning at the gym may strike you as his commitment to being healthy and in shape, and glancing at his phone while you are talking won't bother you at all. Do you see how just changing your view, your own perspective, can actually change the reality of how you see him, which in turn will shift your attitude, which can't help but change how you treat him?

Our mind is a mysterious, extremely powerful, part of us. There have been studies upon studies regarding this. You can create any reality you want in it. From birth, we are conditioned to accept the story that's given to us as "true". Some of our memories are made up of what really happened, some parts come from what you think happened, and some actually come from what others have told you happened and you've recreated the sensory parts in your mind. This being said, our perspectives are formed from these memories and experiences. No two perspectives are exactly the same. Not even twins that were raised the same way, by the same parents, having the same experiences, forming the same perspective. Just because it's your perspective, doesn't mean it's the only one that can be right. When you change your perspective, you change your reality.

I like to think of our minds as made up of four circles. The first circle is comprised of "what happened." This typically starts with an event or events, such as a divorce, an argument, or anything for that matter. From that point, our minds create the second circle, which is "what we say about what happened." At this point, our perspectives, upbringing, experiences, assumptions, expectations, and agendas all come in to the mix. This is where we create the "meaning" of what happened. We create the story here. Our ego intercedes here. This is where we try to make ourselves look good. This is where all the judgment comes in, the excuses and falsities, our ideas of how or why it happened, and it all happens without our overt thinking. It happens more or less automatically in our minds, the process of how we will experience and tell the story to ourselves and others about what happened. Our minds live about 3 percent in the first circle "event," and 97 percent in second circle, "story." Story has tremendous capacity to be false, or at least far from infallible. Two separate perspectives on the same events *can* be sincerely believed, but very different indeed.

The third circle now comes into play. This is where we *attach an emotion* to what we say about what happened. It's chaotic in here. So here's where we feel fear, anger, elation, sadness, happiness, excitement, nervousness, all of our emotions. In that fourth circle, we *react to what we feel* about what we say about what happened. Usually there is a fight or flight response that takes place. We either stay in the emotion and defend it, or we avoid it. Maybe we freeze up, or perhaps we try to bargain with it. Remember, we are not planning our way through these circles. Our minds are doing this all undirected. How we dealt with the entire situation, story, feelings, and reaction, now feeds back into to first circle, as it is stored safely in memory and will be triggered to self-reinforce the cycle the next time something similar happens. Here is a scenario to explain this:

- First Circle (truth): Two people get a divorce. They were married, and now they're not married. There was a legal certificate, there was a legal process to render it no longer valid, and now that legal structure is gone.

- Second Circle (story): They both list the reasons why their divorce happened to their friends and family, being careful to protect their own egos. According to story, he is a jerk, she's too crazy, he never tried, she got possessive, he played too many video games, she spent too much money, you can honestly go on and on here. The conclusions drawn, and the social conditioning all comes in. A story is created by both sides.

- Third Circle: (emotion) She is very sad and lonely. He is angry and frustrated.

- Fourth Circle: (reaction) He goes out and parties every night to release all that energy, she leaves the country in hopes to avoid experiencing the pain.

The only real truth out of all of this is that there was a marriage, and now there's not. The rest is just made up of perspectives. His parents don't think he is a jerk. Her friends think she deserves way more. It's really not as loaded as we make it. There is diversity in how we individually see things. We aren't always wrong, but we're certainly not sure to be right, and we should not over-trust this part of our process. Jeff and I call this "chatter." If either of us has some second circle stuff going on, and we are aware that it's just that, we will say to each other, "I'm having some chatter about...." That's a really good way to say, "This is my stuff, not yours, but can you help me through it?" So we will talk it out, knowing that the chatter could be true or false, and we clear it up pretty quick. Even though we both know what it is when it enters our minds, it still appears because we are conditioned to it and it's a natural part of being human to have that happen. Understanding it, and being aware of it, makes all the difference in the world.

I think of the life that's behind me, and how significant this would have been to know. How many situations could I have gotten through differently with an understanding of my own perspective, and how many issues could I have avoided because it was people's stuff I didn't need to get involved with? I try not to think about it, since I'm always teaching others to move forward, and not dwell in the things we can no longer change. Not an easy task for sure. But can you imagine, if each time something happened that upset you, you could pause for a moment before reacting to it. Ask yourself, "What if my perspective is just that, *my perspective*? What actually happened?" I'm telling you, if you can do that *for yourself*, your entire world will start to open up. It just becomes larger. Throughout our lives, many of us are conditioned to believe that there are only two categories of events or action, "right" and "wrong." So, everything that transpires in our lives has to be put into one of these. If our perspective maintains that we are right, and who doesn't want to be right – then the only other option is "wrong." Perhaps we believe the other person must be right, and blame ourselves for being in the "wrong" more often than we should. Either way, our need for "right" drives a lot of how we handle conflict and dissatisfaction. We fight so hard to stay in something that doesn't necessarily serve us, because if the situation, or the other person is wrong, then we cling to the perspective that it has to be made right.

What if there was a third category? A category called "just is." What if most of your relationship issues were put into that category? There's no longer a "right" person and a "wrong" person, or way of being, or situation to be in. It just *is what it is*. It's ok for a person to stop loving someone else. It's ok that a person decides that they don't like being treated a certain way. It's ok just the way it is. If a relationship no longer serves one of the parties, then it's no longer the same relationship, and that's going to be ok. Imagine if you could look at life, other humans, and events that way. What if different perspectives were the only things that we saw? It's not really truth when you look at it that way. It's just a perspective, maybe someone else's truth, but not something for us to change. Since all of our perspectives are different, then there really isn't a right or wrong way to see anything. So I want you to add this other category, the "just is" category. More times than not, things that other people do and say will fall into this one.

Now think of how you can apply this to your man. What is your perspective of him? Is it *right*? *Wrong*? A little of both? Could you look at his actions, or reactions, another way? Could you maybe even see *him* from a different perspective? Could it be that you have been the one seeing things from a second-circle perspective all along? When you change your perspective, you change your reality. What reality do you *want*? How do you want to see him? Do you realize that you can see him however you want to see him? The power is in you. It's all you.

Another way I like to look at life is like a clock. I learned about this in my muscle testing class, as taught by Steve Brinton. It goes way deeper than this, but this one simple metaphor can help you change your perspective. Think of life as a clock. At 12 we have the truth. What is, what happened, true self, hard facts, objective reality, however you want to see it. At the 3 o'clock, you'll have what's called "the managers." These are the personalities that are on top of everything, always active, never have a spare moment to think for all the doing. These are the perfectionists. At the 9 o'clock, there are the self-destructive people. Drug and alcohol addicts. Sex addicts. Victims. These people live their lives destroying themselves, and they despise these 3 o'clock people who do everything perfectly. The 3 o'clock people don't care much for the 9 o'clock people either, because they should be doing something with their lives instead of destroying themselves.

Now look at the 6 o'clock position. Imagine that the 6 is where all the "yuck" falls. All of the negative experiences, the deception, the misfortune. The stuff no one wants to handle or deal with. By being a 3 o'clock person or a 9 o'clock person, you are able to shove and keep down all of that stuff that causes hurt and confusion. In essence, these two contrasting personalities are created to do the same thing. Avoid pain. The only way to deal with this stuff is to let it surface and work through it.

We often think that as soon as we can stop struggling with what we know as our problem, we will be good. Like that's it – work through our immediate obstacle, and then we're good. But life isn't like that. That's not why we are here. I look at life as a very large, long roller coaster ride. There will always be ups and downs. I've thought that if I can have more ups than downs, that would be great. Even the incline, the anticipation, is a positive thing, though I have been around the track long enough to know that what goes up will go down, and often quickly. If we can anticipate that there will be downs and the sooner we can get through it, we start climbing again, our perspective will change. Think about that roller coaster. If we accept that we will feel and have to experience the fall, then we are immediately propelled back up the track again at similar speed and it feels exhilarating when that happens. So take the downs as they come, learn to embrace them and take them head on.

I don't remember where I heard this first, but it has always stuck in my mind, the only way around your problem is to go straight through it. If you are a 3 o'clock or 9 o'clock dweller right now, but you want a breakthrough, you can let the 6 o'clock stuff come up, be worked through and become part of the 12 o'clock position. If your perspective is that you will take the downs, and turn them into ups as soon as possible, the downs won't be so bad. You may even be able to somewhat look forward to them, knowing that at the end of this ride, you will have learned, grown, and become a better person. If you change your perspective, you change your reality.

I met a woman named Jodi at the gym, and we became close quickly. She had recently moved to town to start over. She had suffered in a bad relationship for years, and needed a break to regain herself. At the time, Jodi lived in an apartment with her cat. It was very clean, her life was scheduled, and she had a routine to follow each day. She was feeling pretty stable in life after this period of reset, and decided it was time to start dating. Or at least she thought that it was the right thing to do – certainly according to all of her friends and family. Jodi would then go on a date, do her due diligence to satisfy that social expectation, and then get back to her perfectly well constructed life. Until she met a man who was a little different. One day, Jodi started telling me about this guy she met, had gone on a date with, and was feeling a bit frustrated afterward. Mostly, that she actually enjoyed his company! She would try to find something wrong with the fellow each time she went on a date, but soon realized that she was becoming smitten with him.

On a particular day we took a drive together, Jodi seemed upset about him. I had asked what was going on for her, and she had explained that the time she was spending with him was causing her to be less able to keep her place as tidy, spend as much time with her cat as she needed to, over achieve at work, and besides all that, she was getting behind on her TV shows. She felt super chaotic in her life, and she was about to call it off with him. I got super excited and said, "Chaos is beautiful!" This means that you are allowing yourself to live again. She wasn't having any of it, and couldn't understand how I could see this as anything but the unraveling mess that it was. I explained to her my theory about the clock. How she was a 3 o'clock person, and that she had created this tightly controlled space around her to keep her safe after her last relationship. While she may have thought she had dealt with her past and was living happily, she had actually been building artificial walls around her existence, created her routines, and lived in this perfect little box, to save herself from being hurt or vulnerable again. I told Jodi that the chaos was a symptom of her finally allowing herself to live. The chaotic feeling wrapped around that allowance was bringing all kinds of anxiety and stuff up for her, because it was poking at what was not resolved from her past. If she allowed the chaos in, she would actually have to deal with her stuff! And if she had to deal with it, she feared her world, as she knew it would come crashing down all around her again.

As we worked through it over the next couple of days, Jodi was able to acknowledge the carefully constructed box that she had created, realized that it had served its purpose, thanked it for protecting her, and then said goodbye to it. She has become a new person, full of happiness and excitement for the future. What a beautiful thing to see! Jodi was able to identify her perspective, see it from a different view, and move forward with an adjusted one.

Where do you sit on the clock matrix? Do you see some or all of these personality traits in yourself? What if you could break through these and allow some stuff to come up? Even a little bit at a time, what if you could embrace it, feel through it, and get rid of it? Imagine the space that you could open up within yourself. Living in the present, unbeholden to the fears and stories created in your past, takes some effort.

In the present, if something positive happens, we file it in our past. If something negative happens, we file it toward our future. If a negative present scenario does not get worked through and turned into a positive experience, it will continue to show up as fear or reaction in our future over and over again – until it's finally dealt with and then filed in the past. Make sense? Most people live in the pain of the past, or fear of the future. The more you can deal with things as they come up, in the present, the more space you create to develop the future that you want. Being aware of your thoughts, seeing the world as a myriad of perspectives, and knowing that you have the control over what perspective you want to have, is such a powerful place to work from. Again, when you change your perspective, you change your reality.

Four Circles

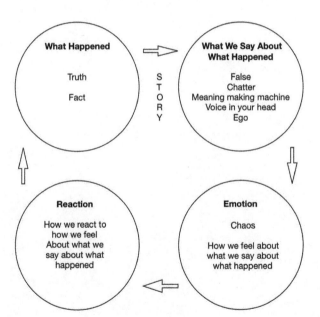

We are here 3% of the time

We are here 97% of the time

What Happened

Truth

Fact

S
T
O
R
Y

What We Say About What Happened

False
Chatter
Meaning making machine
Voice in your head
Ego

Reaction

How we react to
how we feel
About what we
say about what
happened

Emotion

Chaos

How we feel about
what we say about
what happened

Chapter Four

The Divine, Womanly Role You Play

"Being a sweet, soft, loving, kind, and supportive woman will make you the most powerful of all beings. It's sexy and beautiful and magical."

I remember talking to my teenage girls about their feminine role in dating. They truly had all the control. Whatever boundaries they set for themselves, are the boundaries with which the relationship would live within. If they allowed a boy to get handsy or be inappropriate with them, that's how he would learn to treat them. But if they set firm and clear boundaries from the beginning, and told the boy exactly how they wanted to be treated, that's what they would get.

There was some questioning and some opinions, of course, from all three of them. My stepdaughter challenged the idea as much as possible, and soon found out from her experiences that it was truth. Having been taught and tested on setting expectations, she was better able to deal with any situation she found herself in from then on. My other two girls set boundaries from day one and were able to control the pace and intimacy levels of their dates, without pressure. My oldest married a great man, and she told me one of the reasons she chose him was because he always honored her boundaries when they were dating. That set a precedent of respect, consent and communication for their marriage, and it has been super successful so far.

Truth is, I emphasized that because I grew up knowing nothing about setting boundaries because that was not taught in our home. I recognized that if I had had better boundaries I would have known to stay out – or get out – of painful situations. My mom was severely abused as a child and really didn't discuss love or relationships with us as kids. She taught us some basic principles: for example, that God was good, the Devil was bad, and that we wanted to do way more good in the world than bad. She taught us to be kind to everyone, to help those in need, and to protect children and animals. She taught us that money made people bad, and imparted an attitude that we would probably never amount to anything in life. She stayed home with us, was always there, and spent her life tirelessly serving us.

My mom also feared everything. When I say everything, I'm not exaggerating. She feared life. She never drove. She would always tell us a story about how she drove one time and a semi-truck passed her. She felt the wind from it, pulled over and *never, ever* drove again. She rarely did the grocery shopping as a result, and when we didn't have a washer or dryer in one of our many short-term homes, my dad was the one that took the clothes to the laundromat. My mom feared lightning storms, too much heat and extreme cold. She feared cars and cliffs and airplanes. She even feared the microwave. When we finally got her first one, when I was 25, she would push the button and then hide behind the corner until the food was done. My mom feared doctors, too. She passed away of a heart attack at age 67 because she refused to go to the doc.

It wasn't until after her death that I learned a great deal of her tragic story. She herself had been subjected to all kinds of abuse from birth. She was split from her siblings and put into foster care by the age of 6, and spent her childhood passed around from home to home in the system until she met my dad. She had no one consistent in her life; no one invested enough to teach her how to be in a relationship. Somehow, without knowing how to love or how to set boundaries, she gave me some core tools to survive, have compassion towards others and a desire to break the mold and be the pioneer who changed the destiny for my own family. I was on a mission, from a very young age, to not become like this woman that I loved so dearly. Little did I know back then, her divine role on this earth. I wish every day, that I could tell her how much I love and appreciate what she taught me and how she helped to shape me into the woman I am today, as I have come to possess so much love and understanding for my womanly role.

Growing up with a stay at home mom meant she was always at the house. Always. When we woke up, when we fell asleep, and when we got home from school. Breakfast was always there when it was needed and dinner was on the table at 5pm sharp – every single day. I think we were the only low-income family around that had a spotless house at all times. She was the typical June Cleaver-style mom. No matter how poor we were, whether we lived in a house, apartment, motel, or car, she did all that she could to make sure that we had our necessities met.

What I don't remember getting from her was touch and affection. I believe she loved to the best of her ability, given what she had been given. My most precious memories of my young life were when I was ill. She would hold me on her lap, and I would put my head on her chest. She would carry on talking with whomever she was with, and I would feel the vibration of her voice. I remember that feeling like such a safe place for me. I know now that's why I ended up being sick a good part of my life. The mind is a powerful thing. In those moments, I felt loved. My inner story associated being sick with receiving love.

While that wasn't the best thing to take into adulthood, it made me aware that there had to be more stories that would be empowering and positive, ones that I may want to consciously cultivate so that I could give my children the best of what I had been given. I distinctly remember putting those moments, ones in which my mother's love or presence made a difference, in my tool bag of life to pull out later when I had my own kids. When I searched my memory of my mother and something I saw that I didn't like, I would make a mental note to never do that. At first I was on a search for that special feeling of "love." The unconditional, primal kind that comes from a mother.

I know that the seeking of love, after my parents and I parted ways, put me in some precarious predicaments in life. I craved it. I would literally hold on to every speck of it as I gathered it. I loved love. I still love love. That's why I didn't stay in a marriage when I felt the love was gone. Back then, I didn't realize how much influence I had over that. If I did not feel it between my partner and myself, I just felt the need to get out of it and to find it elsewhere. There is no better feeling in the world than to love and be loved. In fact, it is a basic human need. When it comes to humans, there is no better person to spread that love than a woman. We women were biologically built to nurture. We can grow another human in our bodies for heaven's sake! Our breasts can continue to nurture that new life. Our hormones promote bonding, tenderness, attachment, and empathy. Our bodies were fully made to create, nurture, feed and care for other human beings. What a beautiful, divine role.

When I say divine role, I am personally speaking from a Christian, godly perspective. You can use whatever higher power you believe created women. I do know women were created for a special purpose. We were created differently than men for a reason. I remember losing several babies during pregnancy, and how hard that was on me emotionally and physically. I actually carried four of them to term, and I remember how blessed I felt when they were born healthy. I chose natural childbirth, and I remember experiencing it with a sense of sadness in my heart for men. I was actually sad that they couldn't have this direct experience, and I distinctly remember the transformative feeling birth had for my experience of being a woman – knowing that I had been created to facilitate this beautiful miracle. I felt strong, powerful, and blessed to be a woman.

Our society has worked so hard to pull us away from that role. Women are constantly fighting for what they believe is equality without realizing that they're actually taking a step down to achieve that. Not in the sense that women are better than men, but in a sense that we are better at the female role than men are, better at being authentic women than mimicking men, and men are better at the male role. Modern western culture is seemingly fusing and occasionally switching the roles. I never want to have the role of a man. They experience a lot of pressure to provide and be strong. I love and respect it. Their bodies, their brains and hormonal chemistry are created to conquer. Ours are made to nurture. Don't get me wrong, I believe that men can nurture, and women can conquer, but when we do those things deliberately from acceptance and fulfillment of our divine roles, it's far more powerful.

For instance, I had a client, Shelly, who was severely depressed. She came to me on a referral from a former client, and her starting point was being completely unhappy with her life.

Shelly had four kids, a beautiful home, a husband, two dogs, and a fish. She lived in a nice neighborhood, belonged to a church in which she was actively engaged, and drove a newer car. It took her a bit of time and trust to open up and be vulnerable with me, so we could figure out what was going on underneath all of that unhappiness. I asked her about her day-to-day life, what filled her emotional or energy tanks and what emptied them. How much time did she spend with her family, what kind of hobbies she made time for, etc.

As Shelly responded to all my questions and sketched a mental picture for me of her life rhythms, I was really confused as to what she believed her role was. Her husband had a good job. She also had a job. Her husband would come home exhausted at the end of the day. So would she. He would want her love and attention and she would want his. Neither of them had anything else to give of themselves by the time they got home. They would do some chores together, while dealing with the stress of meeting all the needs of the kids: getting the older ones' homework done, packing the little one for daycare for the next day, cooking, eating, and cleaning up after dinner, baths, prayers and bed. By the time Shelly and her husband would fall into bed, they would both be so tired that they would be asleep in five minutes, and in a few hours, when alarms went off, the cycle for the next day would begin. On nights where they actually had some extra time, they each prioritized TV shows they wanted to watch in order to "wind down" from their stressful day. Intimacy seemed like so much work, and besides, she really wasn't attracted to him anymore anyway. Nor did she feel attractive. She was gaining weight, anxious and rushed all the time, so much so that she rarely took the time to even put makeup on, and felt angry-ish *most of the time*.

During the six months that I worked with Shelly, we realized that she and her husband were in the same roles, if not a little reversed. He had become quiet and allowed her to run the household, since she felt she was better at it. She did the bills and the schedules. He was just *there* most of the time. They didn't make time for deep conversations and rarely carved out time for dates. She and I went over their budget and realized that by the time she paid for daycare, gas, all the food they ate from restaurants, carry-outs and convenience food because there was no time to cook, her work clothes – the costs of maintaining her job – the amount of money she was bringing in wasn't much at all.

We discussed what Shelly felt her role was at home. She said that she felt like she should be helping to support the family. All of her friends were doing the same thing, and they all seemed to be okay-ish. As a result of their work, they got to buy bigger houses, better cars, and prettier decor. Not that anyone could ever come over to see or enjoy the pretty decorated house, since there was not much time for friends or socializing. She felt it was a duty, in a sense, to contribute economically. If she stayed home, she would feel lazy and unattractive to her hubby who loved seeing her powerful in the world. *Or did he?* She was trying to remember the last time he grabbed her and kissed her, or gave her a compliment.

Over the next couple weeks, I had her list everything she did in a diary. And by each action, she was to put an "F" for "filled" her tank and an "E" for "emptied" her tank. Shelly started to become much more aware of herself, her thoughts, and what drove her to do the next thing as she moved through her demanding days. With each weekly call, she was already seeming happier, without even changing anything about her situation yet. As time went, we would adjust her to-do list, and she would be able to get rid of more of the E's and fill that space with a few more F's each time. What Shelly was doing is nothing short of taking control of her life, instead of letting her life control her. One of the things that she realized about herself, in this process, was that she didn't like working at her job. She laid down in bed each night feeling guilty for being a horrible mom. Those thoughts obviously emptied her tank. So did dropping off her littlest at daycare. On the weekends, when she had time with her kids, she had more F's on her list.

Having done the work and achieved some clarity, Shelly sat down with her husband, and they had a very much-needed discussion about what she had been going through. She told him that she was depressed, falling out of love with him, bored in the marriage and felt like a failure all the time. Her husband then shared with her that he had noticed some of those things, but didn't dare bring them up to her – because she seemed to him to be domineering, controlling, and had no tolerance for him. So he, too, was feeling worn out by their relationship. He said he didn't feel like the man of the house, felt no control over his life, and felt unloved. Shelly told him she wanted to try not working. They figured out that if she quit, it wouldn't be so much of a difference in income, because they could shed some expenses. They re-budgeted some things and expected to sacrifice a few of their frequent indulges, and she put in her two-week notice at work.

Over the next three months, she gradually let go of some more E's and handed those tasks over to her husband. She freed up so much space inside of her that she began to feel happy *most of the time*. Shelly started to see her husband as smart and productive. He took over paying the bills so that she didn't have to feel that stress. He felt more confident in himself because he was feeling like the actual man of the house. By the end of our six month coaching relationship, Shelly had joined a gym, lost 35 pounds, was putting in quality time at the kids' school, took a mommy-and-me class two days a week with her toddler, and even looked forward to dressing up for her weekly date nights with her man.

I honestly observed the bigger change taking place in her hubby, without ever meeting once with him. He had become more productive at work, received a raise – and coincidentally, the exact same amount they were left in deficit after Shelly quit her job, he had become more active in both his wife's and the kids' lives, was very open to all of the relationship coaching she and I had done, and was practicing the techniques with her. He had confidence, drive, more energy. His happiness was apparent, and this all made him very attractive to her again. She reported to me recently, that their marriage has never been so filled with love and excitement – and that she looked forward to each day with happiness and enthusiasm. They have learned how to create anything they want out of their relationship. Shelly felt like the beautiful, sexy, empowered woman that she was divinely put here to become, and her man saw her as exactly that. This change didn't happen overnight. It took almost a year. My client was able to shift her entire marriage, her husband, and the future of her children, just by embracing her divine role. No matter how deep in despair you feel right now, or how impossible you think it is for your man to shift, there is always a way.

Obviously, the story above is a generality, not all women want to, or are able to, be stay-at-home moms. Not all women are working solely to pay the costs of working; some are taking the lead provider role due to choice or circumstance. I have a friend who is in training to become a firefighter. She is beautiful, inside and out, strong and very much a woman. She asked what my thoughts were about her wanting to take this career path. I observed that as a woman, she could show up on a scene differently than a male could. A feminine approach may be particularly useful to tend to the people. If there is a woman having a baby, a child in distress, think of how a woman can be uniquely suited to bring empathy, understanding, and hope to the situation! She doesn't have to show up as a man or in a masculine role, she can be the woman that she is and still nurture while being a *badass* on the job when she needs to as well.

When I work with women on an individual basis, I meet them where they are at, and find what true way of being aligns with them. Maybe it's having a career, maybe it's quite the opposite, they just want to nurture their families. Maybe they genuinely want both, although they may have to emphasize one or the other in different strengths at different times. But once I can find the true expression that aligns with them, I can better address the effect a career may be having upon their relationship and discern the best way to move forward productively.

Regardless of where you are and what aligns for you, you can embrace who you are and you can shift your man to be supportive rather than resentful or oppositional. Some men can shift with their woman out of the house, being powerful in their own right. No matter where you are in the world, how powerful, strong, independent, and in charge you are, when you walk in that door at the end of the day, you can also choose to let it all go, and be kind and sweet and receptive in your marriage. Step into the role of your man's woman, however the two of you choose to define that. It's a different kind of powerful. A different kind of strength. You can take off his shoes, compliment him, make him dinner; whatever it is that would fill a need for him and allow him to feel nurtured and affirmed. It will cause a shift in him that will make him want to do the same for you.

These are just a few examples. This divinity is in every woman. The working woman can find it, the stay at home mom can find it, the single woman, the woman that never has children. The key word is *woman*. We have a separate place in the world from men, a place that is worth occupying. Once you master it, you will be able to love fully, get rid of expectations, agendas and assumptions, and actually meet your man on a different level. One of an equal kind. Not equal to a man on a man's terms, but *an equal being* as you are both living into your separately powerful roles, serving and loving one another. This starts with you stepping into your role as a woman. Your man won't be too far behind.

Chapter Five

Whatever You Do— And Say

"Communication is the essence of a healthy relationship."

I was talking to a young, married girl named Christi the other day, and she told me that she had an "amazing" marriage. They have been married for seven months, and she couldn't be happier. She said, "The only problem that we have is that we don't communicate very well."

Of course, in my mind, a million red flags went up. Despite her present happiness, all I can foresee with a challenge like that is a future full of resentment and issues. A relationship will not work without communication. Period. This entire book is really all about communication style and communication encouragement. There are so many ways to communicate: You can speak, give a look, listen, touch, use body language, in essence, no matter what we are doing, we truly can't not communicate. Then why does it feel so difficult to communicate with a person that you spend an inordinate amount of time with? In this way, men and women are virtually different species. They could not be more different. If you watch small children, what mostly comes out of little boys' mouths when they are engaged in play are noises. Not anything that makes sense, just noises, like grunts and groans, and bangs and snarls. Little girls will use their body language a lot more, if not their words. They will cuddle and rock and even bite or hit before they will make those strange noises that come from little boys. I remember sitting at breakfast with my two oldest kids one morning, when they were really young. Kenzi, my daughter, set her Barbie doll next to her cereal bowl. Carter, my son, reached over and grabbed the doll, turned her upside down, cocked her leg, pointed it at Kenzi – and pretended to shoot with her, bang-bang-pew-pew-pew sounds and all. I swear, to this day, Carter had not seen a show or movie that glorified shooting, nor had he any experience with guns. I feel like guns were invented by little boys!

Something else I have learned over the years: a man's mind is compartmentalized. I think about it metaphorically as his mind is built like a house. There are many rooms in a typical "house." In one "room" he puts his job, another room the car, in others he puts the boat, the dog, the kids, golf, football, and finally there is a room for you. As with being in a house, he isn't able to occupy more than one of the rooms at one time. Sometimes he is in the golf room, and then heads to the boat room. Sometimes he just wants to sit in the job room, and think about it. When he is in your room, he is in there fully and you get his attention. Sometimes you may metaphorically walk into the football room, and when you try to speak, get shooed away. Maybe your feelings are hurt for the rest of the day. He was in the football room, though, so he couldn't possibly be thinking about your feelings being hurt! When he does get back to your room, he is baffled to find you all sad and frustrated with him. What happened?

The woman's mind, on the other hand, is built like a pile of spaghetti. All noodles lead to one thing ... him, actually. So if your car is broken, or the job is particularly hard, or the kids are on your last nerve, somehow he should automatically know this and come to your rescue, right? At least notice and express some care, you would think? Nope. He can't possibly understand what you are going through, because he has been fully occupied in the football room! I've spent so many hours explaining this one concept to my girls, when they were left disappointed after a date or after their guy cancelled on them or forgot about something, because they weren't on their mind exactly at the right time. It certainly isn't intuitive for us women. This is also a difference that a man needs to be aware of, so that he can make a sincere effort to visit your room as much as possible to check in, and make sure nothing is off balance. I can teach you some ways to help him learn how to do this.

The Power of "Want"

How many times have you given a hint to your man to try to get him to do something or remember something? For example, "Hey, do you know what is going on in two weeks?" or "Hmmmm, I wonder why today feels like such a special day?" What if you just said, "Hey, our anniversary is coming up. I really want it to be a special day, can we do something?" No coyness, no beating around the bush, no expecting him to already know the answer – just ask the question, straight to the point.

This is what men want. They aren't mind readers. They aren't looking through a crystal ball. They are just men and they have not a clue what you want from them until you tell them. How often are you frustrated or angry with your man about something he *didn't* do or say? How often does your man even know what you wanted done or said in the first place? I have heard this from almost every single man I've come across. They all say that if their woman would just tell them what she wants or needs, they would be so much more willing to give it to her. Women go wrong when they assume a man's mind works as theirs does, and even that men would have similar needs so theirs ought to be "obvious."

Jeff and I have had many conversations about this. I'm extremely open about everything. I'm not very good at hiding a feeling, want or need – at all. So I often just blurt out what I'm going through at that moment. If I'm feeling overwhelmed with love, I tell him. If my feelings get hurt, I tell him. If I'm insecure or jealous, I tell him. If I'm staring at him because I can't get enough of his hotness, I just tell him. If I want something from him, I ask. In full disclosure, this hasn't always worked out in my best interest. There is such a thing as too much of a good thing. It's probably good to add that considerate timing is very helpful when being completely open with your man. But I promise, more times than not, they really appreciate it!

Men Are Fixers

Give a man a problem, and he will try to solve it. Give a man something that remotely seems like a problem, and he will try to solve it. Vent to a man about something that doesn't need fixing, and he will try to solve it. Men are fixers. It's in their DNA. This is another area that communication comes in handy. As long as you say, "I just need to vent something, don't need it fixed, just need it to be heard," you have a decent chance of him not trying to fix it. You need to know this, because if you are like a lot of us women, you are plenty capable of fixing your issue, it would just feel nice to be heard. Maybe you even interpret his "fixing" as a statement that he doesn't think you are capable enough to fix it yourself. Just use your words, and it will save you both a little brain usage and misunderstanding.

Have you ever complained about your body to your man? That will lead to four reminder calls, six texts, and several inquiries that week about finding or going to the gym. Am I right? Now you have your feelings hurt, and all you want to do is eat a brownie. In all reality you didn't want him to tell you how to fix your body, you really wanted him to say nothing and be present to your feelings, or better yet, tell you how much he loves your body. This is a good thing to keep in mind when you want your man to listen to what you have to say.

Disagreements

Touch is such a powerful tool. It is our first developed sense. It really breaks down barriers and pride. Touch has been known to help preemies grow, mitigate pain, and show emotions faster than any other sense, it can bring people closer, release the relaxing hormone-oxytocin to promote bonding, and so much more. Touch is an amazing way to communicate, and sometimes it is the simplest, especially when we don't know what to say or do to make things better.

When Jeff and I have a disagreement, he tends to want to shut down. That's how he fought in his last relationship. The argument would start, he would shut down, and he wouldn't have a voice in the matter. Though this was his own pattern and his own doing, this would lead to constant frustration. Now, if he starts to shut down on me, I take him by the hand, sit him down, literally climb on his lap, put my hands on the side of his face, and say, "Don't you shut down on me, babe. Come back. Talk to me." I kiss him on the forehead, make him look me in the eyes, tell him I love him. This isn't always easy, especially when I'm upset, but I do it. All the time. I have to reconnect to him in this way, using touch and physical engagement. Then we can start to talk about what we disagree on. I let him know that I understand how he must feel, share how I feel, we talk it out. Then we either come to agree, or agree to disagree. Sometimes we know there's more to work through on the subject, but we can at least both acknowledge where we are at that moment. Usually he will end up saying something like, "I love fighting with you." Then we kiss and make up.

Funny thing is, he now does the same thing to me if I start to shut down about anything. We've made it a rule in our relationship, that we never argue, or have a major discussion, without touching. In our case, I like to actually sit on his lap and get as close to him as possible. It allows as little literal space between us, or ability for either of us to "run" from the issue, and besides the connection makes us feel closer even if our minds are driving us apart. Sometimes we even start laughing and forget what we were disagreeing over. I'm not saying that you have to climb up on his lap, but I promise you, incorporating touching will cut your disagreement in half, if not defuse it altogether. We rarely leave a discussion unfinished. Sometimes we agree to pause, because it's not the right time to talk about it, for instance we need to give our full focus and we each have other things that need some focus, or we need a little bit of time to think about how to move forward. We make sure we get back to it as soon as possible. One thing that makes me not dread these discussions is, we always bond through our disagreements. Always. At the end of each conversation, we will actually talk about how we feel about the conversation itself as well as the original issue, and we will talk it out until we feel closer and feel complete. We always try to make it a win/win.

What about when you're not fighting? What if every time you walked by your man, you reached out and touched him? Touch his arm, swat him on the booty, brush up against him. Just observe how he responds. You will be pleasantly surprised. This is an awesome way to communicate to him that you notice him and that he's important to you in that moment. It's also a way to be a little playful to lighten a situation up.

Another thing that has become quite clear to me over the years is that any name calling, putting the other down, being mean or disrespectful – even being sarcastic or disrespectful in jest – is detrimental to trying to resolve a disagreement. Neither Jeff nor I approach each other that way, but we have had those patterns in our pasts, and there is a very palpable difference in the feelings during and afterwards. Even the sarcastic humor and the "unintended" putdowns come to erode your confidence in your partner's feelings for you. Those types of statements linger and create more disagreements later. Criticism also has no positive or productive use during a disagreement.

Something I recommend to couples that have been at this for a while, or are feeling particularly stuck, is to take a weekend – or just one night – to get away together. Being in a new place, out of your comfort zone, out of your entrenched ways of being or escaping, can open up some space that hasn't been there before. That space can make the crucial difference toward being able to talk and explore new things. If you can do this once a month, that would be ideal. If it's not a possibility due to logistics, maybe even taking a night out for this purpose only, would do the job. As humans, we form habits. We can get caught up in the daily grind of life and not realize how much of what we are doing is simply a habit. There isn't seemingly time or space in the day for opening up a new subject or activity. Getting away creates a space that's new, therefore new subjects and conversations, and new perspectives can happen there.

Another tactic that really works, although it takes some work to set this one in motion, is to make agreements about how you behave in your relationship. You can have as many as you want. The difference between a rule and an agreement is that a rule implies someone's will is subordinate to the other's. Agreements are statements of what you both believe are important to one or both of you. We have the agreement that we touch during a disagreement. We also have one that we aren't spending time alone with someone of the opposite sex. We do not shut down on each other, and we have to allow the other to speak without retribution. We love having these agreements because they come from a place of wanting to have the best relationship, and we discussed what and how we would handle each situation before or between situations arise when we might need to use them. I really love this idea after reading this part of a poem:

Out beyond the ideas of

right-doing and wrong-doing

There is a field

I'll meet you there

—Rumi, *Out Beyond the Field*

The idea is to find your "field" for your relationship, a place where there is no judgment, a space where both of you can speak without retribution. A place where you can go to form agreements that anticipate the best for, and of, both of you in the relationship. The place or the means of accessing that "field" can be anything you decide on: your bedroom, another room in the house, a porch, the car, wherever you can create a safe space for this. It could be physical as well as metaphorical. I love this practice, and I know it works. Regular use will help you to practice being this "beyond" person at all times in your relationship moving forward, and that is a good thing.

Words of Affirmation

My good friend once told me that she had the perfect relationship, and therefore didn't need to read the book I was writing. She still wanted to know who it could help and what exactly I was going to write about, though. We talked through the chapters and how they cover many of the concepts I teach in coaching.

When I told her that one of them would be on giving compliments to your man, she said, "Yeah, I need to figure out how to do that. My hubby loves compliments, but they are so hard for me to hand out." I asked her why, and she really didn't know. She said it just wasn't easy for her to do. We started talking about how important it is to build up your man, to see and validate what is right with him – and I asked her what she thought could be different if she was able to compliment him twice a day for 30 days.

My friend was like, "I can't even imagine. I could probably get whatever I wanted from him." So with that, I challenged her to do it. I also told her that every compliment *had to be the truth*, or it wouldn't work.

She literally needed coaching every single day to get through the challenge. It was not a natural behavior or pattern for her, and in order to create a new habit, she needed some support. Meanwhile, during and after the 30-day compliment challenge, she really was able to connect with her husband on a deeper level. She noticed that he was far more patient, became more open to doing things with her, and was even constantly helping out around the house, just because he wanted to. Last I heard, she continued the compliments. It became part of her *way of being,* instead of a chore or a challenge. She could easily find reasons to compliment him, and it filled a space in her head that she used to fill with critical thoughts or reasons why she didn't like him. Pretty cool!

I was talking to a good friend of mine, Kade. He told me that his wife could sometimes be harsh on him. She would often yell and seem a little crazy. We were talking about compliments and he said, "I get one of those maybe every couple of months. You know, if my wife would compliment me more, I probably wouldn't mind when she yelled at me." That could have been a bit of sarcasm or at least an exaggeration, but honestly, who knows, could be true also! Kind words can create all kinds of patience, endurance, and love within a soul. Affirmation and positive interactions can create the emotional buffer space for us to deal with the times that things will inevitably be more challenging.

Our words can build someone up – or destroy them. I have, unfortunately, spent a ton of time with women who continuously bicker and put down their man. I'm not sure why this seems to be a trend, but it can be observed commonly in the "wild." For instance, how many times are you in a room full of women and they start bashing their husbands? Or out on a date with another couple, and when the guys are engrossed in something else, the woman starts in on it. *"Guess what my husband did this time?"* I have seen this so many times. It's almost a social contest – like they try to one-up each other with tales of how horrible their man is. I have a few friends who are nurses. I hear from all of them how the side conversation in the OR, or around the break rooms throughout the hospital, seems to always turn into negative conversation. *Why?* Is it because no one wants to listen to someone talk about how *amazing* their spouse or boyfriend are? That makes everyone want to puke, and puking at a hospital is no bueno. Is that it? If one person is miserable at home, *then shouldn't everyone be?* No doubt it feels good to safely vent sometimes, but sure seems like a needless race to the bottom. I've challenged each of these women who work with me to try being positive and choose to speak really kind words about their significant other in a social setting, and see what happens. I'd be willing to bet, if one person holds their ground, the others will start to chime in with positives. No one wants to be left out of a good thing.

I had a focus group running, with a bunch of guys while writing this book. One of the subjects that came up during the communication discussion was that men do not like having a fear of retribution or punishment. I mean, no one wants to have that, but it was particularly sensitive for the men. I asked exactly what they meant by that. They spoke of times when they planned a guys' trip and the women retorted with something on the order of, "Fine, then we will plan a girls' trip." That felt like retribution, or that somehow each person getting something that they *also need and want* – like time with their friends – would be met with some desire to "get even." Instead of seeing that as a win-win opportunity, they were wielding it against each other. The men also felt that they would be judged harshly for their thoughts about things, so they wouldn't express them. They spoke of the "woe is me" mentality, of not having a voice, or the stereotyped beleaguered man being yelled at. Each had different scenarios in which they had experienced it, but all of them had experienced it. I noticed the tenderness in each of them, although they were speaking of these disappointments in such manly ways. Again, communication is everything. If you can allow your man to safely let you know what things make him feel unheard, shut down, or punished – and vice versa – then there can be more honesty and openness, and less fear, between you.

Helping couples communicate is the most rewarding part of my practice. It can sometimes be a challenge to remove the barriers and find the ways that they are best able to relate to each other. Both partners have to commit to it, and have to accept their roles in it. Once we establish better communication practice, it really sets the foundation for all of the other aspects of a healthy relationship.

Chapter Six
An Intimate Craving That Won't Go Away

"When I think of intimacy, I think of two souls connecting...hugging."

I know you've probably heard this a million times: *Intimacy is so important in a relationship.* That's because it's truth. Intimacy doesn't just mean sex. Intimacy means closeness. It means connection. It's what all of us women say we want. We want to feel loved, connected, cherished, thought of, seen – we want to feel that we are someone's entire world.

I did a survey, and asked men and women alike, what are the three most important things they want in a relationship?

Believe it or not, Emotional intimacy was at the very top of the list for *men*! What? How is that? They only want sex for sex, right? Wrong. Intimacy is important for both men and women. *Intimacy is connection.* Connection is such a huge part of any relationship, and there are many levels of connection. Physical, spiritual, mental, emotional, intellectual, psychological, and so on. Each of these has a place, while some can be more superficial than others. Men crave connection and emotional intimacy.

We all know that men are sexual beings and love the visual and physical part of the relationship. But every man I've talked to has also said that one of the most important things to him in a relationship is the emotional connection. Men love to be loved, too. I think of my boys and how close they are to me. When they were small, they just wanted to be loved. They really needed the physical touch. Carter would come across the room, look up at me, and I would know that he just wanted a moment. I would pick him up, or bend down and hug him. He would have gotten his need met in about 30 seconds, and then would run off to play again. Then a couple hours later, he would do the same thing. A moment of connection, of reassurance, of safety. He is an adult now and still loves his mamma. Same with Saber. He hugs me a few times a day, still, and he is a teenager!

Now, I get to address the part of intimacy that makes everyone uncomfortable. *Sex.* Wow, this subject is *the most* controversial subject when it comes to men and women, period! And I would say 99 percent of my clients have an issue with it. I was telling my son Carter that I'm going to have to address this part of the book, and he said, "That's a little too weird for me to be reading about sex from my mom. I will just read all the other chapters." It's funny, sex is the most natural thing in the world, and the common way in which we all got here, but it is such a taboo in our culture. Personally, I love sex. I feel that it's a way to connect with your person. A "plugging in" of sorts. It's a vulnerable place to share love and spirituality. It's also a reward for all that you have to go through in a relationship. I view it as coming together, and not as something I would ever withhold from the person that I love. I hear so many times, with my clients, that they withhold sex from their partners for all kinds of reasons. It's like a grown-up punishment, a "time out," that women turn to in imposing consequences for a man. I also hear reasons why the women don't like it: abuse, trauma, stories from the past, ignorance. I've been through a lot of stuff in my life too. A lot of it needed to be worked through to get to this point. Now, I won't allow anything to take this beautiful, natural part of life away from me. If you have an emotional or physical problem that is holding you back from desiring sex with your man, you should seek professional help. Overcoming this will not only bless your life, but will bless your relationship.

There is no way to have a complete, fulfilling relationship without intimacy, connection, and sex. You may be told that it's possible, and have figured out a way to convince yourself that its true, but I'm telling you, it's not possible. Men are visual thinkers, doers and learners. The number one thing they are attracted to is looks. Men have a need for affection, for physical intimacy. It is a biological need, a requirement for their bodies to even function properly. Society continues to view sexuality as some perverted part of nature that we should be ashamed of, or that we should transcend into some virtuous alternative. Although there are men who have unhealthy relationships to sex itself, for the most part, it's extremely normal for a man to have sex on his mind almost all of the time.

Women constantly complain to me that their needs aren't being met either, and that no matter how uncomfortable it is for the man, he should meet their needs, whatever they are, just because they are the man. Women may feel a need to have their emotional or security needs met before they are comfortable with physical intimacy. At the same time, pride and resistance on both your parts will not move your relationship past the obstacle. So why is it that a woman can't just set some time aside to meet this need for her man? *Go first?* I ask this a lot. For instance, if your man comes to you and tells you that he wants to have sex with you, knowing it's a need of his, would it be so bad to say, "Of course," even if you aren't in the mood? Just like if you were to ask him if he could hang a picture on the wall for you. He may not be super excited to do it, but he will do it, out of love and respect for you. You participating in sex with him, or him hanging a picture on your wall, are part of a practice. To offer one another what they need, if reasonably able, just because your partner asked. It's a good relationship habit to get into. Just like dates and family dinners. It's not just a matter of satisfying his ego. Sex is part of creating a healthy relationship.

I know this is a seriously controversial subject, but a lot of women just say no to say no, to wield some power when they are feeling a lack of some sort. I don't mean to minimize or make light of this beautiful act of love, but I do want to have you aware of it and to maybe have you reconsider the next time. Is there a reason why you can't make the time and put forth the energy to engage in a bonding session with your man? Don't look at it as a chore, or something else he is "taking" from you. Look at it as a part of a whole. Have you thought about the importance of it to his wellbeing, and what it might show him if you are receptive for that reason alone? Have you thought that maybe you need it and will enjoy it, too? Could this one act of service and love be what starts the shifting of your man in other areas? Oh yes, it can be for sure!

Quite often, there is a barrier between men and women when it comes to the physical aspect of intimacy. It goes a little like this from the female side: "My man only seems to be nice to me when he wants sex." "I know he did that chore because he wants sex." "Why is it that all he thinks about is sex?" On the male side, I hear, "She's always too tired or has a headache." "I don't know how to get her in the mood." "She used to like it." Again, it's just perception. Something is in the way, but each side is assuming what the cause is. So think about it, if that's what's going on in a man's mind, remember, he's a fixer. He is going to want to fix it. He thinks, maybe if I help out around the house, or if I'm extra kind, it will fix whatever is keeping her from being intimate with me. It's not a developed manipulation scheme. He wonders what the barrier is, doesn't really know how to identify it, but wants to fix the problem. Women, all too often, get this projection and pride thing going on. They assign the cause, think that if their man is scheming against them, then they should scheme back or not allow him results from the scheme. After a while, the man gives up on trying, and the woman feels validated. However, in the end, both are unhappy and unfulfilled, and too proud to change.

Now, imagine if you could see your man differently. Say he comes home from work a little early, does the dishes, helps with the kids, and you *don't* assume he has an agenda. You look at him and feel gratitude; you even start to see him as "hot." I mean, how many men come home and help their woman? How many put the family needs ahead of escaping into beer, football, or games? When you shift yourself into appreciation, you will feel more energetic, more attracted to him, and way more willing to enjoy an evening in bed with him. Not just because it's what he wants, but because it's what *you* want. You enjoy the night together, feel closer, and fall asleep.

The next morning, you get up and write down ten things about him that you are grateful for. You smile, start your day, and realize that you have way more energy than the day before. This day, you have everything needed for the night done by the time he gets home, since your energy levels are upped since yesterday. That night, he walks in, and sees you on top of life and having confidence from your day. He sees you differently, feels even more attracted to you, wants to help get the kids to bed so he can spend some extra time talking about you and your day before you both retire for the night. You get to connect and bond with a little talk about your day; it feels good to have adult companionship, especially from this man who had become all but a stranger. Suddenly you're attracted to him, and want to feel closer. He is so caught up in the conversation (since you never talk and he feels he doesn't know you), that your advances surprise him. The night ends in a beautiful, intimate moment, and you both drift off to sleep feeling fulfilled. After which, you get up and write down ten more points of gratitude for him. Your day starts with much more energy again. Maybe you even send him a couple texts with gratitude in them. Can you see how this can spiral upward into something new and exciting? It really can start with your shift. With one mindset change. Now I know that some of you may feel like you're too far gone to even think about being attracted to your man again, but I promise – with a change of perspective, some gratitude, and a little practice – it will come back to you.

This particular story is true. It was one of my clients, Robin, who didn't feel she even loved her husband anymore. She wanted out, wanted more. She felt unloved, unappreciated, unattractive. All we did in the beginning was shift her thoughts. That led to shifting her actions and reactions, which shifted her entire way of being. Then Robin's husband started to act differently, seemed happier, more fulfilled, and the more she saw him shift, the more she wanted to shift. One day, halfway through the program, we spoke of all the changes and she told me that she was actually looking forward to being good to him, that she was feeling a lot of love for him. When we change our perspective, we change our reality.

One couple, Madi and Josh, had never really had intimacy in their marriage. They had been married for over ten years, and neither had had a previous, serious relationship. For years, there was nothing between them but friendship and shared logistics. They could rarely communicate without fighting, and touching was almost non-existent. Madi was strong, harsh, and independent. Josh was subdued, defeated, and apathetic. Madi viewed sex as a spousal maintenance obligation, and Josh viewed it as a biological need, and yet it was something so out of reach. Madi rarely complimented Josh or made him feel like he was admired as a man, and was constantly criticizing and belittling him. Josh sought admiration and achievement outside of the home. There was little hope on either side of things ever changing. When he told the Madi he needed more from her, such as respect, love, affection, kindness, etc...she retorted that he needed to just love her for how she was, that she wasn't planning on changing. She told him that she wanted more too. She never felt loved, cherished, appreciated, or fulfilled. She didn't want to have to be the one to change first. She wanted *him* to change first. This prideful way of thinking went on for many years, until Josh moved out and filed for divorce.

This is the kind of story I hear, over and over again. So many of these relationships could be saved and even made better, if someone would give in and *just love*. Now I know that just loving someone isn't always enough, and that our own feelings matter. But if this woman would have taken some time to get to know her husband, to figure out his needs, to see the marriage from his perspective, to get rid of all of the assumptions she was making about his intentions, her heart may have softened just enough to let him into it. And when a woman softens her heart, the entire world can shift. When there is a tug of war of sorts going on, a standoff of personal power, someone eventually has to give. We women are natural nurturers, so we have an inherent ability to take care of others. If we can set aside the pride and the agendas and resentments, and take on our role more fully, we can create peace and harmony, in even the harshest situations. We have the power to shift everything.

Chapter Seven
Serving With a Grateful Heart

*"Service is contagious much like love,
anger, apathy or gratitude."*

J eff and I usually talk on his way to work, on his way home from work, and during his breaks. One particular day, he had worked an 18-hour day, and we had talked throughout the day about something we disagreed on, I honestly can't even remember what it was, but we were both being stubborn about it. On his way home, the subject continued, and he wasn't being his kindest self – for sure – and neither was I. He got home, walked in the door, and sat down on the couch. Usually, I greet him with lots of hugs and kisses when he gets home, but this time, I was a bit upset, so I just stood there. I looked at his face, saw his exhaustion from the day, and I knew that he could really use my love at that moment. So I put my feelings aside, knelt down on the floor, and took his shoes off. He looked at me with a baffled, glazed over expression, and then his eyes filled with tears. Nothing even needed to be said. I got up, sat on his lap, and we held each other for quite a while. I'm pretty sure we've never talked about whatever it was we'd disagreed so stubbornly about ever again. When I asked him later, why he softened so fast, he told me that I served him even when I was upset, and it melted him. Suddenly, whatever we were both trying to win about – became so unimportant. I thought back to that moment, and it wasn't hard for me to do. I love this man, I knew what he needed, and I did it. This isn't the way I behave 100% of the time, but I really try to not allow the walls of pride to go up, ever.

Service is the best way to diffuse any tension, and moreover, to get out of ourselves. The more we serve, the more we are able to see the one that we are serving as a perfectly imperfect human. With that perspective, we are able to love them in a way that isn't possible without it. Try thinking about serving your man. What kind of service would you give to him? When you start to think about his needs, and how you can better meet them, there is a softness that suffuses you. You will start to listen more, so you can hear his needs. You will watch him more, so you can see what his needs look like. You tune in deeper, pay attention to things about him that you normally wouldn't, and discern how he is feeling. Men love to be taken care of. They may not admit it out loud very often, but they truly want nothing more. I believe this is another biological need. So you have a human who needs to be nurtured, and a human who is made to nurture. Seems pretty symbiotic, right? In our society, it's not that cut and dried. Women are made to feel weak in that position, and men made to feel selfish. On the contrary, there is strength in service, and a man that can admit that he is needing to be nurtured, isn't selfish.

I had a client, Karen, a while back. Karen was a mother of five and was unhappy in her marriage at the time. She was referred to me by a dear friend, and it took her a while to be able to open up to me, mostly because of the guilt. She had everything she *should* want. Her husband had a very large income; they lived in a really nice house with all that she could have dreamed of to furnish it. She had five beautiful kids, four boys and one girl. She didn't have to work, so she was able to just stay home and be a mom. When Karen finally opened up, she told me that she thought her husband was extremely selfish. Her husband, it seemed, could basically have anything he wanted. He made a ton of money, at a flexible career, and could command whatever he needed, when he needed it. She had no clue what to get him for special occasions, because he was never in need of anything he couldn't do for himself. She felt inferior, didn't feel she made any contributions to the marriage, and really felt helpless in her own role. She started seeing me when she heard of my work with women and couples, but was very hesitant to believe coaching would work in her situation.

I worked with her over the next three months. We spent a lot of time together, either in person, or on the phone. She really didn't feel much love for this man, and had zero respect for him, when we started. It's pretty hard to shift someone from that place. I decided the best thing for her to do was to begin to serve him. She actually hated this idea, and she almost fired me. I asked her to give this approach a chance, and I even offered to give her money back if it didn't work, which I thought there was a significant chance it may not. I was so sad to see this woman struggle to even *want* to serve her husband, let alone do it. On the other hand, she wanted so badly to believe that she was valuable, that she had some influence and control over the way she experienced her relationship. Her husband certainly wasn't interested in fixing what she felt was wrong.

Each day, Karen would call me, and we would come up with a way she could serve him. The first day, she begrudgingly made him breakfast. She made oatmeal and fruit, without even considering he couldn't stand the texture of oatmeal. It had been so many years since she had considered making breakfast to include him, that she completely forgot that about him. She felt that he was ungrateful for her effort, and he was left confused as to why she was doing it in the first place. She called me in tears, and wanted to give up, right then and there. I gave her a suggestion, and that night she apologized to her husband for making oatmeal. She asked him what his favorite breakfast would be, and then made it for him the next day. She was in much better spirits the next day, and before long, I was actually glad she had made that mistake because it opened up some useful dialog between them. She told him she wanted to be a better wife. He was really receptive, and in return, asked how he could be a better husband. That was achieved on day two!

The rest of the next three months were not all rainbows and butterflies, but Karen definitely didn't want her money back! We worked through some major stuff, and she really started to enjoy serving her man. She felt much better about herself, which he really noticed and appreciated her. I ended up seeing him a couple times as well. I think, to this day, he has been the most grateful client of all. They have new language that they speak together, they both seek to serve each other every single day, and they have renewed a dying relationship. It was beautiful to watch. One of the things that Karen and I worked through revolved around her past relationships with men and her perspective of how she saw them. She was able to have an entirely new perspective after those three months, and given that she is raising four boys, this was so important for their relationships as well. She could love them differently and bond with them more easily, with all of that gunk out of the way of her mindset about men.

Recently, I was asking Jeff how he experiences being served by me. He said this, "Service is contagious, much like love, anger, apathy, or gratitude." I love that so much. It's so true. If we can bring ourselves to serve others, others will "catch" our attitude of service, and many of them will serve us back. I know that the more I have served Jeff, he has in turn served me back in so many ways.

We used to sing the song, "Give said the little stream," to the kids when they were little. We would also tell them that we don't just *share*: we *give*. The word "mine" was not allowed in our house, and was treated like a swear word. The kids grew up to be such loving, giving people. It's simple shifts like this that create a much larger shift in the world. You can start in your own home, with your own people. How wonderful to know that you, a beautiful, divine woman, have the power to create whatever you want in all of your relationships. Beginning, of course, at home.

Chapter Eight
When You Light Them Up, They Brighten

"Look Mom, Mom look, Mom...." I used to think this was the cutest, most special thing ever, when my son Carter was in this stage, even though I heard it 40 times a day! And it was my favorite thing. Little did I know that this was every little boy's mantra in life. When those little boys grow into men, they've been taught to act like adults, so saying things like "look Mom, look wife, or look friend," just doesn't sound as adorable coming from a 35 year old man. So instead, they say things like, "Hey, guess what I did today," or "You're looking at the next CEO," or "Dude, look at my muscles," or even, "Honey, I fed the kids and they're bathed," or just about anything they can announce that seems somewhat grown up and worthwhile, yet still garners some attention and praise.

Just the other day, after talking about this chapter to Jeff, he said, "Come look at this video of me doing snatches at Crossfit!" Immediately, he realized that he was doing what I spoke about, so he laughed and said, "Look Mom, yeah, I'm doing that again, aren't I?" So adorable. It's an art to learn to recognize when he is covertly asking for admiration, and probably doesn't even realize it himself. We all want to be adored and admired, but men, they especially love it. And honestly, they can't live without it. So, if you're not going to give it to him, you can be assured he will find it elsewhere. He will find validation, admiration and respect at work, at the gym, from his buddies, anywhere and everywhere he can. It's a harsh reality. Listen to your man. He is most likely looking and asking for admiration in ways that may not be so overt to you. What you may write off as simple attention seeking has been a natural part of being seen and loved by the people who he trusts to love him ever since he was a tiny boy.

One of my clients, I'm going to call her Jen, hired me because her husband no longer wanted to come home after work. At least it seemed that way to her. She couldn't figure out what she was doing wrong. Over the last year, he had stayed later and later at work. He would often go to happy hour after that with the guys. There was always some project they were working on or some reason why he was needed off hours. He would also pack his weekends with stuff: hiking, mountain biking, car shopping, or to another meeting. He seemed disengaged while at home and just really distant all the time. Jen told me that she thought maybe he was having an affair.

We got a little deeper into what happens at home when he is there, and how they communicate. It turns out that whenever he came home, Jen would hand him a baby, or a broom, or overflow onto him whatever was exhausting her at that moment. All bottled up with her own stuff, she would blurt out her frustration from the day, be upset with him for a myriad of reasons, some rational and most irrational. Weeks would go by without her even listening to him recount his day or what he had going on. All she could hear was the reasons he wasn't coming home.

I painted a picture for her of what it must be like from his view. He goes to work every morning, and while there, he gets complimented, achieves, feels proud of himself, gets attention from women and men alike, feels like a man who is conquering his domain. When he is home, he gets to hear all about the fact that the one person in the world who he wants to keep happy, is unhappy, and mostly *with him*. He feels like a failure, has his energy sucked dry, and would rather be any other place than there. So, given the choice of one or the other, what would she choose if she was in his shoes? She had never looked at it that way. In her mind, he was selfish to want to come home to peace, after she had just spent the entire day working, cleaning, and dealing with the kids. She hadn't really thought that he might be exhausted, too. That maybe he wanted to share his day and receive a little care, too. They had been married in their early 20's and Jen had no clue how a man thought, or how he was different from her. She only knew how she felt, what she felt was expected of her, and projected that all over him. She didn't know that he would need attention, compliments, a feeling that he was doing a good job. She didn't know that she alone could change his entire world. She didn't realize the power of a woman and her words.

Feeling a little more hope, Jen went through my program. She put effort in every day, to change his experience of coming home. She had to retrain him, and his behavior, literally. Unsurprisingly, at first, she didn't see a ton of difference or improvement. But after a couple weeks, then months, she couldn't stop talking about the shift he had made and how she kept wanting to learn more. And guess what? She had shifted herself. Of course, she was only able to provoke that shift in him *because* she shifted her own perspective. She learned so much about herself through this process. She is happier, more fulfilled, and such a powerful woman. Her husband? Well, he works from home now two days a week. He is there every minute he can be. He will still go with his buddies on Saturday mornings and do "guy things" once or twice a month. As for Jen, she encourages it, because she understands his need for male friendship and outdoor recreation. This was one of my most rewarding client experiences.

I started writing a book called *Men Are Dogs*. It's actually about a direct comparison of men to dogs, which illuminates how simple men can be to figure out and to keep happy. I still may finish it someday. Although there were many chapters that had amazing cross references, the premise was really motivated by the ideas in this chapter. A dog's happiness consists of praise alone. I see men in the same way. We either say to our dogs, *good boy*, or *bad dog*, right? What is the dog's reaction to these words? I know that "good boy" usually elicits a lot of tail wagging, body wriggling, and exuberant happiness in a way that is so easy to read if you know anything about dogs. All you have to do is say "bad dog," and the tail goes between the legs, the head goes down, they crouch lower to the ground, and move slowly away.

Do you get what I'm saying? Men may not have tails to put between their legs, but if they did, you bet that's where it would go! I've learned a lot about men over the years, and the one thing that always sticks with me is that they need a lot of "good boy's" to stay motivated.

Words of affirmation are important to the male ego. Men really like to feel needed, loved, wanted, sought after, and admired. A little, "Thanks for lifting that for me. I couldn't have done it without you," goes a long way. I often find myself mothering, as we women are so good at. This only works on the positive, as no man responds well to, "Honey you aren't doing that right. Let me show you." They do much better with something like, "Wow you're amazing, and I loved watching your arms while you were lifting that."

Next time, say, "Babe, I need your guns. I can't lift this." And then watch while he proudly and happily gets up to help. He won't feel nagged like he would if you told him to "Shut off that game and help me move this dresser." Your need for his help isn't any less legitimate than his need for relaxation, but your ability to make him feel good about your request is a big deal. Although the primary attraction for women is the inner characteristics of a man, a man needs to hear that his woman is attracted to him.

Men want to be heroes. We women want a Prince Charming, right? We need to let him be this archetype for us to the best of his ability. It's a win-win. Plus, there are many ways you can praise your man and many things you'll find to praise him for once you are looking. I think about Jeff here, and how much good I see in him. What if every time you see something good in your man, you tell him? I never have to make something up. In my case, my man works extremely long hours, is super strong, he's highly motivated to be a better person, and tries to always meet my needs. He reads books, gets stuff done, runs our home, is an amazing dad, a great provider, is very loving and kind, very handsome, inspires others, I really could go on and on. Again, what do you focus on? What you focus on will magnify and grow. When you focus on the positive attributes and then praise them on what you see, you will have an endless list.

There are so many ways you can show your man that you admire him. Compliments are a good way to show him. Don't just throw out random ones though. Make them count. Be truthful, sincere, authentic. Find something, anything that's the truth, and then compliment him on it. When you start looking for his positive attributes, you will find more than you thought was there. With each compliment and each show of admiration, your man will naturally want to do more and be more, to receive much of the same. Admiration is one of the keys to a man's well being. It's like a plant that needs nourishing soil, some sun and ample water to grow. Without one of these key ingredients, the plant will soon wilt away. A man without admiration will wilt. He must have it. He will find it somehow. The healthiest place for him to find it is with his partner.

One client of mine, Mary, struggled with building her husband up in life. She didn't even know why she had such a hard time. We worked together for a few months, and she started to connect with her hidden perspective: a fear that if she continued to stroke his ego and make him feel good about himself, he would get so confident that he wouldn't see her as good enough for him anymore. We all know that there are some self-love issues going on here, but this was a real fear for her. She didn't want him to grow out of her, or feel he should be aiming his sights higher. She feared that he wouldn't treat her well if he knew how amazing he actually was. So whenever she would see his amazingness, she would stop herself from letting him know how she felt, in fear of it taking her place in his world.

I told her a story about a family night lesson I conducted with my kids once. I took two candles, and I lit one. Then I had each kid take a candle and light their candle by the one that was already lit. I asked them, "What do you see when the candle ignites?" Each one of them was surprised to see that the original flame grew larger while it was lighting the new candle. I explained to them that when we light another candle, our flame gets bigger and brighter. I wanted them to have a visual of how helping others doesn't take from us. It actually nourishes us and makes us larger, stronger, and more powerful. So they should look for all the moments in their lives when they can light another "candle." One of the ways we agreed we would create this, in our own family, was to regularly give compliments.

As I spoke to Mary about this experience with my kids, she began to cry. She realized that she had not only not lit her husband's candle, but because of the fear and the state of their relationship, she had actually dimmed it and her own candle as well. What a harsh reality that was for her. They had been married for eleven years, and she had been doing some of this the entire time. She didn't even know where or how to start fixing the damage, even though she knew it must be done. In Mary's case, we decided the very best thing to do was to sit down and talk to her husband, Jim, and let him know she felt horrible about this mistake she was making in their marriage. That conversation was handled in front of me. She brought him to her next meeting with me, and told him everything in reflection, the things she was feeling and the reasons why she behaved that way. It was such a beautiful moment. Because she had owned up to what she had done, it left a wide-open space for her to tell him of all the things she loved about him over the years. It was an outpouring of praise, admiration, and respect. Jim sat there with a blank stare for a very long time. He soon got weepy and told her that, at that moment, she was the most beautiful thing he had ever seen. He explained that although this was extremely painful, he had spent years wondering what was wrong with him. He felt that it was his wrong doing that was getting in the way, or she would have affirmed and complimented him on his efforts.

This was the beginning of a healing period that went on for months. Because she was brave enough to tell him what she had done, and vulnerable enough to risk admitting why and extending herself to tell her full truth, he was able to communicate all of his feelings about her over the years, too. They went to that field of no judgment, where they both talked and talked for hours upon end. They cleaned up so much stuff that they told me that they felt they were back in high school dating again. Those two have such a cool relationship now. There is a ton of integrity, and Mary makes space every day to compliment her husband. Do you see how Mary created this? How she took it into her own, beautiful, powerful hands and made it happen? When we pause in life, and step back to take a good look at ourselves, and how we are being in the world, endless possibilities to create whatever change we want will open up.

Chapter Nine
We All Get A Little
Lost Sometimes

I remember a time when we didn't have phone navigation, and we had to use a map to get places. I love to travel. Back then, whenever I would get to a new place, I would pull out a local map and memorize it, because I wanted to know where I was and how to get to everywhere else I might need to go from there. What I didn't prepare for was when new roads came, or there were accidents, or construction, or something else that may throw me off the planned path. One time I went on a trip to New York with my daughter Kenzi. We were with a group on a structured tour. I realized that having a tour guide was the best thing ever. I didn't have to solely rely on myself, the map, and a little bit of luck; the guide customized our stops, knew the interest points, and created learning experiences along the way. The entire trip was more enjoyable and easier to navigate, and I've tried to travel like that ever since.

Speaking of travel, on one of my girls' trips, I met Lori, who was initially a friend of a friend. We started talking, and she told me her story about her marriage. She had been married for nine years at that point, and things weren't good. She had read several books on fixing her man, and tried – to the best of her ability – to go at it alone. She had a lot of pride, and was a relatively private person; she didn't really want others to know they were having problems. They had the perfect family image on social media, carefully cultivated to impress on the world that all was well. So she tried a bunch of techniques she had learned while reading. Some weeks she would try hard, some weeks, not at all. In the end, her marriage failed, and they got a divorce. In fact, she had taken this very trip to get away from all the sadness. Yet here we were, talking about it. She asked me if I knew any way that she could have done better. She didn't quite feel like she did her all, and she didn't have any closure about the relationship. I told her about my program, and how I have weekly calls and anytime chats, and help women see some of their blind spots as we work through each situation as it arises. We all start with something relatively small and achievable, so there is a momentum that continues to pick up and motivate during the process. We discussed how this would have been helpful to her while going through what she had gone through. She also realized several things, from our conversation, that amounted to her part in the demise of the marriage. This saddened her, and she feared she could never recover from that loss. Lori is now an ongoing client of mine. She has come a long way since that trip. She has confidence in who she is and how she is being in her relationships. She is happy and lives with purpose.

I wrote this book like a road map. You can see where you are at any given time, but if you don't know which way to go or the exact destination you are trying to reach, it would be impossible to figure out the directions. Life will continue to happen around you, and you will be pushed down one road or the other, that is its nature. Without clear directions, and a strong support system, you could find yourself doing nothing but continuing in circles until you're so tired you have to stop. Don't try to do it all by yourself. You have resources around you. You can lean on a friend who has well-developed relationship skills, a spiritual advisor, or be guided by a coach. There is no doubt that there will be speed bumps in the road along your journey, and an ally on the journey will help you tell the difference between hitting a speed bump and having the wheels come off. I am reminded here of a bit of dialog from *Alice in Wonderland*, between Alice and the Cheshire Cat:

> Alice: Would you tell me, please, which way I ought to go from here?
>
> The Cheshire Cat: That depends a good deal on where you want to get to.
>
> Alice: I don't much care where.
>
> The Cheshire Cat: Then it doesn't much matter which way you go.
>
> Alice:... So long as I get somewhere.
>
> The Cheshire Cat: Oh, you're sure to do that, if only you walk long enough.

How long are you willing to walk without knowing where you are going or being able to tell how best to get there?

Chapter Ten
Creating New Possibilities with Your Feminine Power

*"When a woman is empowered,
the possibilities are limitless."*

W hen you look at the divine woman that you are and recognize that, *as such,* you have power and influence in your relationships, you will feel empowered to begin using it. We all grew up having our divine feminine parts minimized or devalued, but nothing could be further from the truth. There are many women that realize this, but are immature, so they use their feminine power to play head games, to control and manipulate their man into giving them what they want. This can achieve some results, but is not sustainable. It's not authentic, and so it eventually does the opposite of what the divine feminine is about, i.e. building and nurturing a lasting relationship.

While I was going through my learning process, I read as many books as I could on the subject of getting what you want from your man. I wanted to know how. Every single one of them was about playing head games and emotional and sexual manipulation. No joke, all of them. I read that you should not call him back when he calls, make him chase you, withhold affection and intimacy, keep him guessing, be a mystery. This isn't me, or who I want to be caught *being* in a relationship, and I felt frustrated because of it.

All I ever hear from the men that I have interviewed, worked with, and learned from, is that they want someone that is honest and straightforward. Someone that doesn't play head games. They don't want to have to play a guessing game all the time. They don't want to be strung along to react like puppets. This gets exhausting, and although it may be fun and a challenge at first, they really want to just feel intimately close, have great communication, and be admired by the woman they love.

Women have needs, too. My wish for you is that you have them met. When listening to the needs of women, I hear a few common things. "I want him to listen to me." "I want him to understand me." If you can communicate well with your man, these needs will be met. Another thing I hear a lot is, "I want him to be attracted to me." "I want him to quit flirting with other girls." "Why does he stare so much at other women?" "I don't feel like he is committed to me." Intimacy is the common problem area attached to these statements. Makes sense, when you think about it. If a need isn't getting filled by the person who should be filling it, it's going to get filled elsewhere. Not an excuse for this type of behavior, but a reality for sure. The other thing I hear a lot is, "I want him to come home more." "I want him to want to spend time with me like he does with others." "Why isn't he as attracted to me as he used to be?" A man who doesn't feel admired by his woman, struggles with just being around her. Remember, admiration, or at least affirmation, is a need. You can't expect your man to fill your needs if you're not filling his. It definitely goes both ways, but you actually have more influence than he does when it comes to creating change, because you can think holistically and you can start from a place of nurturing rather than conquering. What causes the seed to germinate and flower to bloom? It isn't conquering.

When a man's needs are met and he is fulfilled, he will *want* to do the same in return, and you won't have to do anything artificial or deceptive to bring it about. Be your best self and treat him with kindness and affirmation. He will shift. I like to think of this change process on the man's side as building a machine. Once you learn about how to put it together and get all the parts working, you can turn it on and it runs on its own. As with any machine, there needs to be care and maintenance. You need to offer it regular check-ups and be able to notice the warning signs of it beginning to strain or break down. If you take really good care of it, it will last for a very long time.

A Letter from *My* Man, Jeff

This world is a wondrous playground. We are born into families, taught how to conduct ourselves as men or women by our caretakers, and then embark into the world with aspirations of finding happiness with others. People come and go in our lives, and often times, we allow our relationships to develop or shape who we are without any thought of our role in the relationship that we created. We have the potential to create blissful harmony or, as many of us have experienced, something far less desirable.

I love that this book has made it into your hands. It speaks to your intention of creating a better relationship, a better life, and an improved perspective of yourself. If you are wondering if you are capable of an upgraded even idyllic relationship, I assure you that you are. We all are. We all have access to kindness, service, and love, the core ingredients to a healthy, mutually serving relationship. Sometimes these timeless characteristics get obscured by heartbreak, negligence or sense of entitlement, but we still have them. As we remove the barriers that hold us back, love who we are and what is, we begin to experience life with gratitude and joy. From that space, our relationships hold an improved purpose and serve everyone that experiences us.

Prior to meeting Shirley, life was seemingly good. I had three beautiful children and a rewarding career in the medical field yet felt something was incomplete. I felt my only value to my family was to provide a paycheck and a safe place to live. It seemed the only way for me to serve my family better was to work more, which took time away from being a husband and a father. I didn't consider my potential to be anything more than a plutonic husband in a mutual exchange of logistical family responsibilities. I didn't see how my experiences had me believe that I was a poor communicator, inadequate partner, and to accept a life that was far less desirable than I was capable of. At that point, I reached a crossroads in life. Continuing the way things were going was no longer an option. Reconciling with my ex-wife proved to be something I no longer believed was in the children's or our best interest. The decision was made, divorce occurred, and I set out to be a different man and a better father than I had been in the past.

When Shirley and I started dating, I found the space to be me. I started paying attention to thoughts, emotions, and reactions that I had covered up for years in efforts to keep peace in the previous relationship. I discovered that I was not the person I was portrayed to be: selfish, unloving, workaholic, unsympathetic, undeserving. Characteristics that sabotaged me from my true being. Self-worth was restored, and with that, came confidence and freedom to love unfiltered and unconditionally.

Shirley and I now thrive in a relationship where there is space for each of us to express our needs, desires, concerns, and ambitions in a mutually accepting way. There has been no need to keep secrets or withhold our perspectives for fear of retribution. We have created a space to accept and love each other where we are at as individuals, which is to love things as they are and embrace reality, not the idealized version of how our partner should be.

It is a beautiful thing to witness as Shirley has been introduced into my social circles. She brings a light and perspective to people that they might not have ever considered before in their relationships. I've seen casual dinners turn into life-changing conversations where people are able to look within and take ownership of their experiences and relationships for the better. She comes from a place of love and desire to serve that is felt by all those who meet her.

Today, I am an improved human being, and sharing this journey with Shirley continues to be blissful. I still have a past, still have experiences that I cannot change, but who I am going forward is up to me and up to each of us. Shirley has helped me to see things in myself that I was incapable of seeing in the past. In addition to my children, she is life's greatest blessing.

We all have a path to travel, experiences to have, relationships to create and a life to live. Without clear intention, these experiences will occur in spite of our insecurities, barriers, and incomplete ability to create the best outcome. Shirley possesses a heaven-sent gift to help us remove our self-imposed limitations to create powerful results in life and in our relationships. The life we want is ours to create. The choice is yours.

Acknowledgements

Where do I start? With my kiddos, Kenzi, Carter, Graycee, and Saber, you cheered me on, believed in me, gave up time with me and put up with my constant, "I'm writing a book," excuses so I could get this done. My little Angel Isla, you give me smiles and sunshine every time I need it. Addie, Xander, and Troy, for allowing me to enjoy loving little ones again. My parents for everything. Misty, my daily inspiration, my guide through the blocks and breakdowns. Kyle, for keeping me (or trying to keep me) aligned, Billie, thank you Sis for letting me go incognito for a spell – and thanks for the unconditional love. Merijo, you are the friend that is there no matter what, for over 30 years and counting. Gina, my sanity, my life coach and you don't even know it! OM, you have inspired me more than you will ever know. To my ex-husbands, for being a part of my growth. My supporting friends and family on Facebook and at the pool. Katrina, Jill, Nolen, Leanne, Karla, Jael, Chris,

Cammie (you will be missed), Shayne, Ruth Ann, Tony, Krissy, Terry, Boni, Joni, Ginger, Nancy, Annette, Robert, and Lewis. Grateful for you all. Thank you is not enough, but thank you!

To the Morgan James Publishing team: Special thanks to David Hancock, CEO & Founder for believing in me and my message. To my Author Relations Manager, Bonnie Rauch, thanks for making the process seamless and easy. Many more thanks to everyone else, but especially Jim Howard, Bethany Marshall, and Nickcole Watkins.

Thank You

Thank you so much for reading my book! I love that you continued to the end. It shows me that you really do want something different in your relationship and that you're willing to take the first steps!

It's one thing to realize your potential. It's another thing to put all of these tools into action. I want to make sure you're seeing great results so I've created an **Are You Getting What You Want Quiz**. It's a simple way to check in with yourself to see what's working for you and what's not.

You can get your copy of the **Are You Getting What You Want Quiz** at getwhatyouwantfromyourman.com/quiz

About the Author

S hirley is an entrepreneur and Success Coach who has devoted her life to serving others. Over the past 15 years, her clients have included MLB players, celebrities, children, women in transition, and couples. She has a passion for empowering people to embrace their divine self and have the love they deserve. Shirley has a magical ability to love and connect with individuals on their level. She lives in Gilbert, AZ with her soul mate, Jeff, and their blended family.

Morgan James
Speakers Group

www.TheMorganJamesSpeakersGroup.com

We connect Morgan James published
authors with live and online events
and audiences who will benefit
from their expertise.

Morgan James makes all of our titles available
through the Library for All Charity Organization.

www.LibraryForAll.org

CPSIA information can be obtained
at www.ICGtesting.com
Printed in the USA
BVHW082343130819
555817BV00001B/4/P